Shortcuts to

bouncing
back from
heartbreak

Other titles in the series:

Shortcuts to
bouncing back from heartbreak

Gael Lindenfield

Thorsons

Thorsons
An Imprint of HarperCollins*Publishers*
77–85 Fulham Palace Road,
Hammersmith, London W6 8JB

The Thorsons website address is: www.thorsons.com

and *Thorsons*
are trademarks of
HarperCollins*Publishers* Ltd

First published by Thorsons 2002

1 3 5 7 9 10 8 6 4 2

© Gael Lindenfield 2002

Gael Lindenfield asserts the moral right to be
identified as the author of this work

A catalogue record of this book is
available from the British Library

ISBN 0-00-710054-X

Printed and bound in Great Britain by
Omnia Books Ltd, Glasgow

To Cheryl Buggy

With love, admiration and hope
that you never have to bounce back again!

Acknowledgements for the

Shortcuts Series

First, thanks again to all the people who have so openly shared their struggles with me. I hope that you will be pleased that the wisdom I gained from your difficult experiences has been constructively channelled into these Shortcut strategies.

Secondly, many special thanks to Jo Kyle who has done such a magnificent job with the editing of these books. Working with Jo in cyberspace has opened my eyes up to the amazing potential of electronic relationships. I have learned to trust and respect the judgement of someone simply through the exchange of written words. (A good lesson for a writer!)

Thirdly the Thorsons team have been as patient, supportive and willing to experiment as ever. A big thank you to each and every one of you.

Finally, once again my husband Stuart's contribution must be acknowledged. The title of this series was his idea. As ever, I am also grateful to him for his giving over so much of his precious free time to editing my dyslexic manuscripts before they leave the privacy of our home.

Contents

Introduction to the
Shortcuts Series

At this moment in your life, reading a book is probably one of the last things you feel like doing. If so, you are exactly the kind of reader I had in mind when I designed this Shortcuts series!

I have struggled with enough personal problems myself to know that when you are in the throes of them, the thought of wading through any book is daunting. You just haven't got the concentration or the motivation. When I am in this situation, all I long for is for someone to tell me what to do – or, even better, relieve me of my hurt or worry by taking it away from me!

So I would like you to think of these Shortcuts guides not so much as books, but as supportive *tools*. I do not intend them to be like an absorbing 'read' to take to the sofa or bath and get 'lost' in. On the contrary, they are designed as 'ready-made' strategies to help kick you into action – and to keep you moving over a period of one or two months – at least! (Isn't 'the getting going' always the hardest part of solving any problem? This is when I have found that even the most competent and self-reliant people can benefit from support.)

But it is also important that when we do get started, we begin in a *constructive* way. A common mistake is to *do* the first thing that comes into our mind. This can make us feel better because we *feel* more in control. But this 'hit and miss' approach often gets us going on a very much longer and rockier road than we need have taken. In contrast, this series will guide you along a route that has been meticulously planned. The Shortcut strategies are derived from years of experimentation and studying other people's tried and tested paths.

The first characteristic of each strategy that you may notice (and perhaps find initially frustrating) is that they all start with some preparation work. This is because, in my experience, diving headlong into the heart of the problem often proves to be the shortcut to failure!

After you have prepared yourself, the strategy moves along in a series of small steps, each with its own section. Although sometimes these steps will overlap, most of the time you should find that one naturally follows on from the other. At the end of each, you will find a list of tips called 'Action time!' Some of the suggestions and exercises contained in this section may work better for you than others. But I am confident that in the process of trying them, you are much more likely to find out what *will* help than if you did nothing at all! So I hope you will find them of use one way or another.

The steps also contain some quotes and key 'messages'. I hope you will find these useful should you just want to dip into the book and gain some quick support and guidance at times when the going feels tough.

Finally, I would like you to always bear in mind that in the personal development field there are no prizes for being first to the winning post. But there are, however, plenty of rewards to be had from the *effective* learning of problem-solving skills. So if you proceed through these Shortcut strategies at a pace which feels **comfortably challenging**, you will have learned an invaluable skill that could save you time and energy for the rest of your life.

Enjoy the journey! (Yes, problem-solving *can* be highly pleasurable!)

The greatest power we have is the power of choice. It's an actual fact that if you've been moping in unhappiness, you can choose to be joyous instead and by effort, lift yourself to joy. If you tend to be fearful, you can overcome that misery by choosing to have courage. Even in the darkest grief you have choice.

The whole trend and quality of anyone's life is determined in the long run by the choices that are made.

NORMAN VINCENT PEALE

Introduction

You have lost your love. So right now I guess you must be feeling sad, lonely and possibly quite desolate. The chances are that you are also feeling physically and mentally exhausted. Perhaps the last thing you feel like doing at this moment is bouncing back into the world!

I know this vulnerable state well. I have had my own heart painfully crushed several times. Also, through my work as a therapist, I have witnessed many hundreds of others live through the same kind of deep hurt. I know that the task of climbing out of this 'black hole' feels impossible, however super-intelligent and super-successful your head (and others) may try to remind you that you actually are.

Emotional pain is a great leveller of people. It can play havoc with our minds. It jumbles our thoughts and diminishes our capacity for concentration. It causes even the very best of minds to go frighten-ingly 'blank'.

And as if we hadn't problems enough at such a time, heartbreak also stresses out the best of bodies! It robs each and every sufferer of their usual supply of physical strength. Even the fittest of athletes can feel drained of energy.

Is it any wonder that so many of us feel powerless to help ourselves?

If ever you start putting yourself down for *needing* to read this book, remind yourself that you are not alone! Millions and millions of heartbroken people throughout history all over the world have felt just as helpless as you probably feel now.

But the great news is that some strong survival urge in you has already kicked in. It has guided you to pick up this book. It is urging you to believe that however deep your hurt and however many times your heart has been broken before, you *can* and *will* recover.

I expect someone (if not hordes of people!) has already quoted, in one form or another, the popular saying 'Time is a great healer'. Perhaps you don't believe them and that was one of the reasons you began to read this book. If so, that's a great start! This book is much more likely to be of benefit to people interested in self-help than to fans of the 'Let's just sit it out' approach.

I don't believe that time has any magical powers to heal a broken heart either. In fact, left to its own devices, it can do quite the opposite. I have seen many people become unhappy, cynical and depressed because they have sat back and waited, and not taken any active steps to treat their emotional pain.

So it is indeed good news that you are treating your emotional pain with the seriousness that it deserves and you have already started to do something to help yourself.

But a word of warning to those of you who might have been attracted to the word 'Shortcuts' in the title of this book. Although I will be showing you the *fastest* route to recovery, there are no instant cures hidden amongst the pages of this book. This is especially true if your relationship has been very long-standing or your loved one has died. You may find that you need to follow the stages of this strategy over as long as a one- or two-year period. Some of you may also benefit from having the support of a counsellor while you are working through the strategy. But even those of you who have been less severely wounded will need to give this book more than just a quick skim read. As I said in my introduction to this series, I have written these Shortcuts guides as 'working' tools to be used over a period of one to two months. This little book is designed to help kick-start you into positive action. But it will only do so if you 'DO' as well as read! If you want to stay on this fast track back to emotional health, sometimes you will have to summon up a good deal of effort to try out my suggestions. Some suggestions, of course, may not work at first and you may have to try them several times before they have an effect, and some may work better than others. So please think of this book as a supportive guide rather than an infallible oracle. Never lose sight of your own inner wisdom. (Yes, it will surface once you get into action!) Although the book is packed full of suggestions from those of us who have successfully healed our hearts, it is not an exhaustive collection. You can, and undoubtedly will, discover many more en route. Emotional healing, even more than physical healing, works best if it is individually tailored.

Are you now ready and willing to commit yourself to healing your heart?

If so, read on. A new life and a new you are awaiting your arrival!

Time will not heal your heart without your help.

What is the
Shortcut Strategy?

As you will see, our Shortcut strategy for bouncing back from heartbreak is divided into three stages:

STAGE 1: Preparing Yourself
STAGE 2: Healing your Heart
STAGE 3: Moving On ...

As I mentioned earlier, within each of these stages there are a number of different steps to work through. If you give yourself adequate time to work steadily through all the practical steps in the three stages, I assure you that your heart will emerge stronger than ever.

It is important to work through the steps in the order I have suggested, and it is also important not to skip steps (or at least not to skip reading them through to check whether they are relevant to you). Sometimes there may be some overlap, but generally speaking the strategy should roll gently along in a forwards direction. If, however, you do find yourself getting stuck, there is nothing to say that you are not allowed to backtrack. This is *your* heartbreak and you and only you are director of your recovery strategy.

This strategy has been derived from the experiences of many thousands of heartbroken people who have already bounced successfully back into the world of love and romance. Isn't it true (though a bit of a bore to accept!) that even on shortcut routes we arrive more quickly and safely at our destination if we take the tried and tested paths?

The three stages

In **Stage 1** we will look at some ways to ensure that you are physically, mentally and spiritually in good-enough shape for the healing steps in Stages 2 and 3. This stage will also help you adjust your lifestyle to ensure that you have adequate time to deal with your heartbreak.

For those of you who are particularly keen for a high-speed recovery, this stage may feel frustrating. Rebuilding your emotional strength, however, is similar to any other building project. The foundations are never the most interesting part of the construction but, unless they are laid with care, all other work is likely to be a waste of time and effort.

Stage 2 is the core stage in our healing strategy. To begin with, you will explore your hurt with a view to working through the emotions it has triggered. Then you will learn when, and how, to receive comfort from others, how to compensate yourself for your loss, and how to put your heartbreak into perspective.

By the time you reach **Stage 3** the intense pain of your loss should have abated, and you should be ready to put your heartbreak behind you and move on with your life. So, in this section you will find many tips on how to fortify yourself emotionally and physically, as well as on how to take those initial crucial steps back into the world of love and romance *if* that is what you decide you want to do.

A final word

When working through this strategy, please remember to go at a pace that is comfortable and easy for you to manage. You will notice that I have not included specific time guidelines for completing each step. This is because it is impossible to generalize about how long individual people will need to finish the suggestions and exercises in each step. This is not just because we are all so unique, it is also because our lives and their pressures vary so much. As I explained earlier, I would expect the majority of people to take one to two months to complete the whole strategy, but let yourself be one of the exceptions if you need to be so. What is important, however, is that you set yourself an outline timetable and mark this in your diary (for example, note down at least an anticipated finishing time for each step). In order to be able to do this, you will also need to set aside specific periods of time in which to try out the suggestions. A period of two hours a week would be the minimum amount of time you would need to allocate to your self-help work. Otherwise you will lose momentum and motivation.

Although this Shortcut strategy demands effort and time, there are lots of suggestions for indulging yourself both physically and emotionally, so you should have some fun doing it, too!

> **Emotionally damaged hearts can be as hard to heal as those which have been physically strained. A simple strategy for recovery will make your task both quicker and easier.**

**If you have the courage to love,
you survive.**

MAYA ANGELOU

Stage One

preparing yourself

Like most other activities, emotional healing work is usually much more effective if you have prepared yourself well beforehand. This stage will show you how to free up the space in your life that your healing needs, and it will also help you to de-stress your body and mind and ensure that they are working as 'efficiently' as they possibly can be during this difficult time. Although you may be longing to move more quickly onto the core of this strategy in Stage 2, please take enough time to do these preparations efficiently. Trust that this valuable underpinning work will save you time (not to mention further angst!) in the long run.

STEP 1

Live in denial for a while

You may think that this is strange advice from someone who, as a therapist, spends most of her time encouraging people to do the opposite!

So why this exception to the rule?

Quite simply, we need the recovery 'space' that denial gives us. 'Nature' invented this particular psychological defence for a very good reason. When we receive the shock of any severe loss, our nervous system automatically switches our bodies into 'emergency mode'. Whether we like it or not, hormones are produced which trigger a cycle of physiological responses.

The set of responses that 'Nature' (or whoever!) designed specifically for coping with loss is commonly referred to as 'freeze'. When these begin to 'kick in' we often find that our limbs feel literally frozen to the spot where we are standing. We find that we cannot walk or even talk. Our eyes go still and we hardly blink. Emotionally, we also feel numb. If asked what we are feeling, we commonly reply 'Nothing'.

Some people often unkindly berate themselves for not responding to their rejection or desertion in a more assertive or even angry way. Others are surprised by the fact that they didn't even shed one tear. But our primitive response mechanism knows what is best for us. It knows our emotional limits. It knows that on top of the initial stress the bad news brought, our bodies cannot stand the additional degree of pain that the full reality of our heartbreak will bring. That's why we find ourselves propelled into this temporary state of stillness. It is also why we need to allow ourselves to live in denial for a while.

It is quite natural after the initial shock of your loss to behave as though nothing had happened. People who are bereaved act similarly. You need a period of time to allow your body to return to its normal functioning mode. You are not avoiding the issue.

You are merely preparing yourself to face it and cope with it.

> **You are not avoiding the issue when you're in denial for a while – you are preparing yourself to face *and* cope with it.**

Of course, some of you may not have found yourself naturally being propelled into 'freeze' mode. Perhaps you immediately flew into an uncontrollable rage against your lover or their new loved one, even though you may not have wanted to do so. Like the woman who recently made the news by giving away her husband's vintage champagne collection, you may have been sorely tempted to do something you later would regret. (Vintage champagne tastes wonderful!) Alternatively, you could have turned away and fled the scene. I have known people whose immediate response to their hurt was to turn away from their jobs or their families who they needed and loved.

If you did respond with a 'fight or flight' response instead of the 'freeze' one, there is undoubtedly a reason embedded in your unconscious mind which will explain why you did so. Perhaps your 'natural' response to heartbreak was conditioned by early childhood experiences, or your inherited temperament makes you more likely to respond with anger or fear, or, indeed, your hormonal balance has been disturbed by recent stresses.

But NOW is not the time for you to reason why! Right now your priority is to **give yourself a break!**

Obviously, our denial must have some limits. There will be all sorts of practical reasons why you cannot continue to live your life exactly as before. This is especially true if your loved one was very much part of your everyday life. Also, you may find that you are not capable of taking on as much responsibility or physical exertion as you normally can. But, nevertheless, within these restraints allow yourself as much denial as is realistically possible. Most people need a few days but some need as long as a week or two.

> **It's okay to kid yourself that all is well for a while. A little dose of denial at this stage can be good for you.**

**He was awake a long time
before he remembered
that his heart was broken.**

ERNEST HEMINGWAY

Action time!

- **Take control of your conversations** – don't initiate ones about your heartbreak for a while. Instead, get in first with other subjects before your friends have a chance to ask about it. If they don't 'get the message', tell them you will appreciate talking it over at a later date.

- **Don't destroy the evidence** – as tempting as it may be to clear the decks of reminders of your relationship. Keep their picture up and their clothes in the wardrobe (if they are there).

- **Keep to your everyday routines as much as you can.** You need the stabilizing effect they give you.

- **Use positive self-talk** – repeat phrases to yourself such as 'I'm fine' / 'I'm calm' / 'I'm enjoying this sunshine (or this cosy fire!)'.

- **Find some absorbing useful activity** – this will divert your attention from the pain of your loss, but also will give your shaky self-esteem a mini-boost. This could range from spring cleaning your office or kitchen to redecorating a room or redesigning your garden.

- **If you feel it necessary, tell 'white lies' to yourself to 'explain' their absence** – use your imagination to help you carry on as though your loved one was away on a temporary break.

STEP 2

Allow yourself
time to heal

Most people find themselves quite naturally shifting out of denial. When their bodies and minds have sufficiently recovered from the shock, they find the reality of their new situation gradually begins to seep into their consciousness. Commonly they begin to wonder about their ability to cope with their loss. As a result, feelings of anxiety and sadness begin to mount. In an effort to 'take control' of their emotional turmoil, they often throw themselves into busyness.

You may already be aware of how you have been protecting yourself from the pain of your loss by keeping yourself fully (if not over) occupied. Your diary may well be more than usually full. You may not appear to have any time to spare to do the emotional healing you need to do. But if you are truly serious about wanting to recover from your hurt, you *must* clear up some space in your schedule.

At first you may well resist this idea. That's natural. Who wouldn't rather be engrossed in an absorbing and diverting activity rather than facing the pain of heartbreak? But sooner or later nature will force you to find the time anyway. As we discussed in Step 1, a dose of denial in the early stages of heartbreak can be good for us, but running on denial for any length of time will put stress on our bodies, which will result in them tending to 'cave in' under the pressure eventually.

> **Isn't it better to make a conscious decision to heal your heart when *you* want to and do it at a pace that suits you?**

Another risk you take if you don't schedule in time to deal with your heartbreak is that denial can become a habitual way of living and being. I have seen this happen to too many hurt people. Following on from the very natural stage we have just discussed, they begin (in an unnatural way) to also deny that they *need* or *want* to love and be loved. And, commonly, they will also use their busy schedules to bolster this conviction. Perhaps you have met such people too. You might recall them talking like this:

> 'No, I'm fine. I never even think of him/her – I'm much too busy. I can't think how I ever had time for a relationship anyway. I'm much better on my own, doing my own thing in my own time, in my own way. It was a blessing in disguise when he/she left.'

Sadly, when something does eventually make them face the real truth about their needs and wants (such as the birth of a friend's baby, a close shave with death, or simply even a 'soppy' movie) they find they are locked into a lifestyle and behaviour habits that can take a long time to shift.

The good news is that with our Shortcut strategy, when you shift yourself out of denial you won't be plunging yourself straight into your hurt. You still have quite a bit of preparing yourself to do yet before you move on to the healing steps in Stage 2. But even that won't start to happen unless you give it some space in your life.

Recovery takes time, attention and work. There is no easy way to lose someone dear to you or something meaningful to you.

BOB DEITS

Timesaver chart

Tasks (next two weeks)	priority rating	usual hours	minimum time
Food shopping	1	2	2
Washing/ironing	2	2	1
Visit Mum	1	5	4
Dog walk	1	5	4
Homework	7	3	1
Tax return	2	3	2.5
Research flights	1	1	0.5
Clothes shopping	8	4	1
Gardening	7	2	0.5
Letters/emails	4	3	1
Totals		**30**	**17.5**

Total hours available for healing = 12.5

Action time!

- **Draw yourself a timesaver chart similar to the one on page 27.**

  - in the first column list as many of your main commitments over the next two weeks as you can remember. (You can add more later as you think of them.) Include not only those in your diary but also the everyday routine ones which are not usually listed.

  - in the second column give each commitment a priority rating using a scale of 1–10.

  - in the third column enter the normal amount of time you would spend on each activity.

  - in the fourth column (bearing in mind the priority rating you gave each commitment in column two) enter the amount of time you could save by either not doing that activity for the next two weeks, doing it less frequently, or cutting a few acceptable corners while doing it.

  - total the amount of time you have entered in column four. This is the amount of

time you have freed up for healing your
heartbreak.

- if you think you need more time for
  healing your heartbreak, return to your
  list and shave off some more time from
  your other commitments.

- **During the next few weeks, make a
  conscious effort to 'think and question'
  before doing routine tasks.** By giving
  yourself 'treats' and cutting back on the
  amount of time you spend on certain activities, you will find that you can effortlessly
  store up hours of 'scrap time'. (For example,
  cutting short phone calls / sending fewer
  emails / treating yourself to a taxi instead of
  waiting for a train or looking for a parking
  space / ordering a meal from your favourite
  takeaway restaurant, and so forth.)

- **Go to bed 15 minutes earlier each night
  and get up 20 minutes earlier in the
  morning.** By shifting some of your late after-
  noon and evening chores to the early
  morning, you could double that extra five
  minutes that you created by getting up

earlier and have a whole 70 minutes extra healing per week. (Yes, even the owls among you can work faster and more efficiently after a night's sleep!)

- **Explore ways to delegate some of your routine tasks.** If you briefly explain what you are doing, you should find people very willing to help with doing things like shopping, babysitting or even helping out with a work project. This would also be a good time to consider treating yourself to some practical, professional help at home. Could you afford some help with chores such as cleaning, gardening, car washing or decorating for the next few weeks?

- **If you still have some holiday days left from work, why not allocate a few half days to work on this strategy** – you will enjoy the rest of your holidays much more when your heart is healed.

STEP 3

Nurture your body, mind and spirit

You are stressed.

Perhaps you don't need me to tell you that – but then, maybe you do!

Even when people are aware of the strain their heartbreak has put them under, they don't necessarily treat their body, mind and spirit with the delicacy they deserve.

Commonly, this is a time when people bother less, not more, about taking care of themselves. Indeed, it would be highly understandable if, for example, you now find you are not eating as well as you would normally do, or you are skipping your evening classes, or forgetting to do your daily meditation.

Your body, mind and spirit all need more, not less, nurturing NOW!

The healing steps that we are going to discuss in Stages 2 and 3 will demand energy from all three of these sources. So even if you don't feel much like giving yourself some extra 'treats', force yourself to! It is an essential preparation for your later 'treatment'. Take as long as you can, and as long as you need, before moving on to Stage 2. Hopefully, then your increased self-nurturing will become a habit you won't *want* to break – ever!

Your body, mind and spirit all need more nurturing – NOW!

The most profound relationship we will ever have is the one with ourselves.

SHIRLEY MACLAINE

Action time!

- **Fill your fridge and store cupboard with highly nutritious, easy to cook food,** and make sure you have some healthy nibbles and snacks ready at hand. Lock away anything that might tempt you to binge and leave you feeling guilty and possibly fatter! Your self-esteem needs building not knocking. (For example, my favourite snacks are ready-washed fresh raspberries and strawberries, cooked asparagus tips, and small smoked salmon and rye bread sandwiches. I would lock away my non-healthy favourites – the chocolate digestives and fatty cheese!)

- **Replace some of your brisk showers with long, scented bubble baths in candlelight.** For a truly relaxing experience, add a few drops of an essential oil of aromatherapy to your bath – oils such as chamomile, clary sage, frankincense, jasmine, lavender, marjoram, neroli and rose are wonderful to use when you want to stop the world and float away.

- **Switch off all the trashy TV programmes that you wish you were not watching!** Unless there is an alternative programme that you really love and enjoy, make yourself a nurturing drink and read a light novel or magazine. (No, sorry, the drink shouldn't be your favourite alcoholic tipple – that could bring up feelings you don't need now! Stick to something like a special tea or a freshly squeezed orange juice.) Alternatively, ring a good friend who you know will be supportive for a chat, or do some stretch exercises to the sounds of your favourite uplifting music.

- **Make your going-to-bed routine longer than usual,** and ensure that it is an especially nurturing time. Finish your day by doing a relaxing activity such as reading a light novel, listening to quiet music or having a leisurely aromatherapy bath. If you find your mind keeps wandering back to depressing or sad thoughts, take control of it by doing a simple meditation exercise, such as the one that follows:

A Quick Positive Visualization Exercise

(Try this whenever you cannot sleep or whenever
you want to switch yourself out of a negative
emotional state.)

1. Lie or sit in a comfortable, well-supported position. Close your eyes and concentrate on the flow of your breath. Imagine that as it enters your body it is a warm orange colour and that as it leaves your body, it is a pure iridescent white light.

2. While continuing to visualize these colours, gradually deepen and slow down the pace of your breathing until your body is feeling deeply relaxed and your mind has started to 'float'.

3. Use your imagination to take you to one of your favourite relaxation spots – this could be a comfortable sofa or your garden, or it could be a more exotic location such as one where you spent a peaceful, happy holiday (without your lost loved one, of course!). Notice and enjoy all the scents, sounds, colours and textures of this special place and

imagine the serenity and beauty of this place seeping into the pores of your skin.

4. Focus your mind's eye on one object or aspect of your scene while continuing to breathe at a gently rhythmic rate until you feel even more deeply relaxed and glowing with positive energy. When I do this exercise, I visualize our garden in Spain and I focus my mind's eye on a beautiful fountain which is in the centre of the garden.

5. If you need to get up and get going again, take your time to 'come round'. At the very least, do some gentle stretches and take a couple of slow deep breaths before rushing back into the world again.

- **Beside your bed, have some simple treats ready in case you are awake at night**. Your sleep may well be disturbed. Instead of lying awake brooding in the dark, pour yourself a hot drink from a pre-filled thermos (but make sure the drink doesn't contain caffeine), have a couple of biscuits while listening to your favourite relaxing music, and/or read a light or absorbing book or magazine.

- **Ask a friend to check from time to time that you are keeping up with most of the hobbies, pastimes and sports that you usually enjoy.** If your heartbreak has left you without a partner for your activity, find a replacement (but not a new lover – yet!). If you can't face your usual location (the same pub, restaurant or health club), find a substitute even if it is not your ideal.

- **Take a daily walk that brings you into contact with nature.** Consciously contemplate the beauty you can see, hear and feel around you.

- **Make sure you have at least one vase of fresh flowers in your home and/or office** (even one bloom will do if a bunch is not possible).

- **Join a gentle exercise class** – tai chi, yoga or pilates would all help to ease the tension out of your body and will not demand too much socializing from you.

STEP 4

Take stock of the 'knock-on' effects

Often the end of a relationship doesn't just mean we lose one person out of our life. It often means we lose contact with other people who are dear to us, such as our ex's family or their friends. Sometimes it can mean a loss of income or even a home. Occasionally, it can mean a change of job as well.

Adjusting to change at the very best of times is difficult. It is stressful in itself. Even exciting adventures present challenges that are difficult to work through both practically and emotionally. The cliché 'Human beings are creatures of habit' is true. It is natural to feel less secure and less competent when our routines are altered. In five years time you may well be looking back at this period in your life and thanking 'the universe' for every one of these changes. But, for the moment, it is more likely that you are berating it for plunging you into apparently unmanageable chaos.

Now you are in better physical, mental and spiritual shape, it is time to start doing some serious thinking about your future. It is important that you do this analytical work before moving on to Stage 2 and opening up to intense feeling once again.

Putting the following action points into practise will help you feel more in control because they will temporarily divert your attention away from your feelings and re-energize the rational thinking centres in your brain.

> Heartbreak doesn't just hurt our heart, it also disrupts our life. Don't become a victim of the changes it brings. Stay in charge of *your* life.

The day he moved out was terrible
That evening she went through hell.
His absence wasn't the problem
But the corkscrew had gone as well.

WENDY COPE

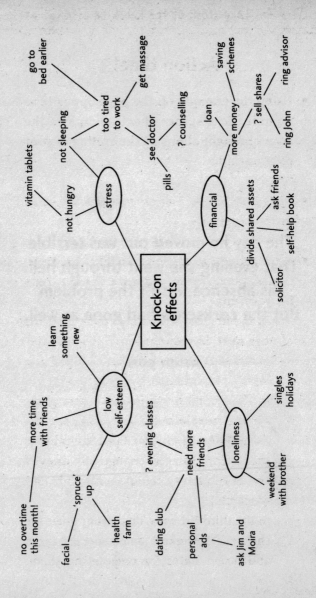

Action time!

- Using the example on the page opposite as a guide, do a spider chart to explore the issues brought about by the ending of your relationship.

- Ring the major issues and list them in order of priority.

- After reflecting on your list of prioritized issues, make three separate 'To Do' lists for yourself:
  - in the first list write down your goals for **the next 12 months** – use general categories such as new job / new house / new lover / new friends.
  - in the second list write down your goals for **the next 6 months** – add approximate dates when you hope to achieve them. (For example, change of hairstyle: end of February / rejoin tennis club: end of March.)
  - in the third list write down your goals for **the next 4 weeks** – name specific tasks and target dates for completing them.

> (For example, ring solicitor: 21st February / house valuation: 3rd March.)

Pin these lists up somewhere and forget them while you are working through Stage 2! (Unless some of the tasks such as ringing the solicitor or doctor for an appointment need to be done sooner rather than later.) It is now time to move on to considering the core stage in your healing process. Hopefully, however, the knowledge that you have some ready-made plans for your future will feel very supportive while you are going through the difficult stage of confronting your heartbreak.

Stage Two

healing your heart

Hopefully you are now well prepared and have sufficient energy and time to devote to this the core stage of our healing strategy. Once you have worked through the following steps, you should be well on the way to full recovery. Some of the exercises are not comfortable or easy to do, so make sure that you continue to nurture yourself well and keep good contact with supportive friends.

**We are healed from suffering
only by experiencing it in the full.**

MARCEL PROUST

STEP 5

Explore your feelings

You are now entering the most challenging phase of your healing process. Before starting to explore your feelings, it is important to feel sure that you and your life can, *at this moment in time*, take the extra strain. There never will be an ideal moment for bringing your hurt to the surface, but certainly some times are decidedly better than others.

Start by checking that you are feeling **reasonably fit and healthy.** Of course, it is unlikely that your body will be at its best until your heart is healed, but it would be wise to postpone this part of your healing if you know that it is currently under some temporary strain. So, for example, if you happen to have a heavy cold or you have just broken your leg, wait until you have recovered your normal levels of physical energy before forcing yourself to face your loss. Concentrate your energy on getting better and fitter and continue giving yourself extra nurturing and care until you do.

Similarly, should you be in the midst of any other **personal crises** or **unusual work pressures** such as, for example, your father or mother having been taken into hospital, or your child having just failed an exam, or you having just been given a project-from-hell to oversee, then hold back. You can continue later. In the meantime, don't forget that you also deserve and need extra nurturing and rest.

Once you have given yourself the 'all clear' in both these areas, it is time for some confrontation with reality.

In short, the next step on the road to recovery is to explore your hurt with a view to working through the emotions it has triggered. You may already have a good idea what these are, but equally you may find you are in for a surprise. I know that on some occasions when I assumed my predominant feeling would be sadness, I discovered that it was actually anger that surfaced – and vice versa. So stay open-minded and don't anticipate your reactions before you have explored your emotional depths.

> **Don't pre-judge your reactions. Let your feelings surprise you. One plus about heartbreak is that it is almost always self-enlightening.**

Finally, it is important to work through the following suggestions and exercises at a pace which enables you to still maintain control over your feelings when you need to do so in your ordinary day-to-day life. So, should you find that the exercises, for example, are stirring up so much hurt that you cannot concentrate at work, you may need to wait until you can take a day or two off before continuing the strategy. The last thing you need at the moment is to lose your job as well. That would probably set you back considerably and your heartbreak would take very much longer to heal.

But if you love and must needs have desires, let these be your desires:
To melt and be like a running brook that sings its melody to the night.
To know the pain of love of too much tenderness.
To be wounded by your own understanding of love;
And to bleed willingly and joyfully.

KAHLIL GIBRAN

Action time!

- **Set aside some quiet uninterrupted time to replay significant scenes from your relationship in your mind**. Use photographs or symbolic objects, such as special presents from your loved one, to help recapture the feelings. If you associate certain music with special times, you can also play that. Before doing this exercise you may want to check that a friend or relative or counsellor is available at the end of a telephone or in another room should you begin to feel very sad or angry and need some extra support.

- **Try writing about what happened**. It is important not to worry about *how* you write. This is not a time for composing exquisite poetry or any other literary masterpieces. Remember, this is first and foremost therapy for YOU. So make sure you have somewhere private to keep your 'jottings'. You will then feel freer to let your mind and pen wander where it wants to go. Don't hold back with your language. These notes can be shredded at your will. So, if you want to write down some 'unfair rantings', use expletives or be sentimental and gushing, feel free! Noting down snippets of remembered conversations may help to bring the hurt even more alive. Similarly, writing a 'never-to-be-posted' letter to your ex-loved one can also be useful. (But please try to forget reasonableness and forgiveness at this stage!)

• **Ask to talk through your experience with a trusted friend**. Keep it clear in your mind *and* your friend's mind that your main aim in talking to them is simply to explore your hurt. (They are not there to comfort you or to offer you advice – these steps come later!)

So choose whom you talk to carefully. **You must have someone who, at this moment in time, can and wants to listen to YOU and you only.** So it is usually wise to avoid mutual friends. Not only will they find their divided loyalties may get in the way, you may find yourself more intent on pulling them down off the fence on to your side than doing what you need to do at this moment.

Choose someone who isn't in the habit of jumping in with cheering platitudes or wise-cracks. Similarly, advice and 'straight talking' at this stage are frequently counter-productive. You want someone who can just listen and let you feel what you need to feel, even if your feelings may appear to be irrational or over-the-top.

Be aware that your very good friends may not be able to do this. They could be too full of their own feelings about your relationship. Try to steer clear of the ones who, for example, on seeing your tears are likely to say some-thing like *'You shouldn't be sad – you should be shouting with joy – he/she was a waster!'*, or those who respond to your angry exclama-tions with *'I bet he/she is really cut up about it too. I know you still love him/her – I think it is just sad that it turned out the way it did.'* You must feel free to express your emotions, however muddled and illogical they may appear to be to either you or your listener.

If you cannot think of any personal friend or acquaintance who can maintain sufficient control of their own feelings not to need or expect to have attention in return, seek a professional. Your doctor should be able to refer you to someone you can talk to, such as a counsellor or a self-help organization or group. Even a confidential telephone crisis line, such as the Samaritans, can be very effective for this stage.

- **Although after having a good moan, cry or scream your body should be much less tense, most people benefit from finding additional ways to release tension.** The kinds of feelings generated when these emotional states are intense or prolonged can provoke symptoms such as headaches, backaches and digestive disorders. So it is important to **make sure that you are also doing some kind of physical activities which will help you to release any build-up of tension in a safe way.** Energetic sports such as swimming, squash or running are especially good if you are angry.

- **But do balance these energetic forms of 'relaxation' with the more gentle or passive kind as well.** For example, as I mentioned in Step 3, yoga and tai chi are excellent forms of exercise to help relax the mind and body. This could also be a good time to treat yourself to a massage. Try to make sure that the masseur is a trained therapist, rather than an amateur friend or simply a beautician or sports masseur. You want to be able to tell them in confidence what has happened and feel sure that they can handle any emotional reaction you may have in the session. A trained aromatherapist would be a good choice, as they will also select special oils to help you to release the appropriate feelings.

If massage doesn't appeal or isn't possible, use a self-help relaxation technique at least once a day. (See overleaf for a quick and easy relaxation technique.) If you use a meditation technique (such as the positive visualization exercise on page 36), it will give your mind as well as your body a rest.

A Quick and Easy Relaxation Technique

1. First, give your muscles a good stretch, focusing particularly on the ones you know hold most tension in your body. (As I spend a lot of time working at a computer, for me this is my shoulder and neck muscles.)

2. Next, do a minute of marching on the spot, gradually increasing your pace but not to the point of exhaustion. (Yes, like the soldiers! Left arm and right knee up and then right arm and left knee.)

3. Now take some slow deep breaths, while concentrating hard on the flow of your breath in and out of your body.

4. Next, stand or sit in a comfortable well-supported position. Place the fingertips of your hands together and hold them in an easy relaxed position pointing downwards.

5. Finally, close your eyes and repeat this phrase slowly five times: 'I am cool, calm and in control.'

STEP 6

Allow yourself to be comforted

You may have already moved quite naturally from the last step into this one. Perhaps the person who helped you then is the ideal person to help you now. But often they are not. Hopefully, this will become clear when I have explained what you will be aiming to achieve with this step.

Your job now is to sit back and TAKE. (Undoubtedly harder for some of us than others. Everyone's skill will improve with practice though!)

This is a time when you allow yourself to be indulged and nurtured. The more physical this experience can be the better. The emotional state that you are seeking is the kind you hopefully had when you were a young child. Can you remember a time when, for example, you lost your favourite toy and were being cuddled and cosseted by a sympathetic, warm, trusted adult?

If you can easily recall such a memory, you will find this step no problem. Enjoy yourself!

But if you can't remember ever being comforted in such a way, you could get a little stuck here. I certainly used to do so. Like me, you may not think you need comfort (you are after all one of the world's tough survivors!). Secondly, you may feel awkward with the role of taker (you have probably needed to become one of life's 'givers' instead). Thirdly, you may not think you know anyone who can help you in this way (you might not even recognize such people when you see them!).

The good news is that if you do learn now to accept the reality that you do need as much comfort as any other human being, and that the world is teeming with people both willing and able to give it to you, you will not only heal your broken heart but also possibly a childhood injustice as well. This will mean that you could end up being emotionally much stronger than you have ever been in your life.

So, even if this step takes you a little longer than most people, remember that you have more to gain from it than them!

> **Your job now is to sit back and allow yourself to be comforted.**

**It's the friends
you can call up at 4am
that matter.**

MARLENE DIETRICH

Action time!

- **Find a person to comfort you.** Ideally the person should be someone who truly empathizes with you. When we are sad or angry, isn't it so much more supportive to be with someone who also feels sad or angry because we have been hurt? This is because we are getting other 'goodies' for the 'price' of one. Our spirit, self-worth and values are being rein-forced at the same time as we are receiving our comfort. But, for your purposes now, empathy is a bonus, not an essential. Your comforter could (as with the person who helped you explore your feelings) be someone who hardly knows you. I have known people look up old friends and relatives for just this purpose. (Grannies are favourites – especially those who put on the kettle before asking any questions!)

  Once again, your helper could even be a professional. You may find them working at a cosy nurturing guesthouse or a healing centre, such as a massage therapist, a reflexologist, or even a beautician. But this is not the time to be seeking a counsellor or psychotherapist unless they are willing and able to step out of their professional role and become more like a friend.

However competent you are at looking after yourself, what your heart needs now is to RECEIVE practical nurturing care and/or touch (even a hand on your arm may be enough).

- **Give yourself some comfort.** (Yes, this is in addition to receiving care from someone else!) Even the men amongst you should set aside one or two evenings, or even a whole weekend, to nourishing your body. Switch your phones to their message services and lock yourself away from distractions. Here are a couple of examples of how you could spend your nurturing experience:

    Give yourself a long leisurely soak in a scented bath with a box of your favourite chocolates and a glass of fresh fruit juice, wine or an ice-cold beer. (But beware – any more than one or two drinks could defeat the object by making you sad and morose again.)

    After your bath take time to slowly and gently massage moisturising creams or oils into your skin. Treat your hands to a home manicure. Then prepare yourself a special comforting meal. This could be the sort of

homecooked food an indulgent parent pre-
pares for their child. Alternatively, it could be
a plate of 'haute cuisine' takeaways from a
delicatessen. Whatever food it is, it should
smell and taste irresistible! Light a couple of
aromatherapy candles and curl up on the
sofa with a favourite video. A tried and tested
movie is best for this purpose. You won't
then run the risk of any emotional surprises.
Go for a swim or a run in the park. (If the
weather is foul, do half an hour of exercises to
your favourite CD.) Order a bumper takeaway
meal to be ready when you surface from
the shower. (But make sure it is a least semi-
nutritious! For example, if you can't stand
sushi and it has got to be fish and chips,
double up on the fish and halve the quantity
of chips. Or go for a pizza with extra *vegetable*
toppings.) Sit and eat your meal while soaking
your feet in a basin full of warm water loaded
with aromatic oils. Then give yourself a
leisurely pedicure while listening to a cassette
of a book you have always meant to read.
(Most bookshops and libraries stock these
cassettes and most chemists now stock an array
of products and tools for home-pedicures.)

**It is not so much our friends' help
that helps us,
but the confidence of their help.**

EPICURUS

STEP 7

Give yourself some compensation

This step is particularly important for those of you who have had your hearts wilfully broken or who feel as though you have been 'cheated' in some way. But it should, nevertheless, be a worthwhile part of *anyone's* healing programme! If your heart is broken, your self-esteem deserves some recompense, even if no one is to blame but yourself or fate.

Commonly, people argue that their relationship was 'priceless' and that there is no way any amount of amends could make up for losing their loved one. But remember that your aim is not to go for a 'tit-for-tat' settlement (you can always give that responsibility to the lawyers!). You are working with your emotional health and not your bank balance. Trust that after finding the advantages in your new situation and compensating yourself in the ways I suggest, you will feel psychologically uplifted. You will then move back into your social world in a more positive frame of mind. Then, even if you do not choose to look for another relationship for the time being, you will at least find yourself more able to enjoy the many other kinds of happiness that life can offer.

The kind of opportunities you have for giving yourself compensation will vary with each person. For example, some people will find that the loss of their relationship has left them with vast amounts of time to 'kill'. Others will find that it has done the opposite. For example, parents left to cope single-handedly with their children rarely have enough hours in the day to cope with the practicalities of life. Similarly, some people will find that they now have much more money to spend, and others will find their finances being strained to the limit.

For those of you whose opportunities are now limited, the challenge is to work with the few that you do have and resist the temptation to look over your shoulder at those who appear luckier. You must do this for *yourself* – for the sake of your own mental health and happiness. If you don't, you could experience feelings of bitterness and resentment which will make it more difficult for you to put your hurt behind you and move on with your life.

Instead, why not look for the small amount of recompense you can seize today and cheer yourself up further by planning what you can do in the future when you do have more scope.

If you have been 'knocked down' *you* **have the power to pick** *yourself* **up – and there is no better way to do this than by finding the advantages in your new situation.**

**Our greatest glory
is not in never failing,
but in rising every time we fall.**

CONFUCIUS

Action time!

- **Over the next week or so, notice, appreciate and make a list of the small advantages that not being in your relationship has brought,** for example:

  - I can watch whichever TV programme I want to watch
  - I don't have to worry any more whether he/she will turn up or not
  - There are no more smelly socks lying on the bedroom floor
  - I don't have to make any more Sunday outings to his/her parents!

  Hopefully, like others who have done this exercise, you have found more of these 'freebie' compensations than you ever thought was possible.

- **Take yourself on an 'outing' that you have thought about treating yourself to in the past,** but have rarely or never got around to organizing. For example, go to the cinema / a concert / the theatre / a gallery / some special gardens / a national sporting event, and so forth.

Plan a day trip / a weekend break / a holiday to a country you have always wanted to visit. If you can't face going on your own, offer to take a friend. Explain what you are doing and they will then be more keen to go with you. They would also understand that the price of the extra ticket would be worth every penny to you.

On your return, place the programme or holiday photos somewhere prominent in your home as a reminder to give yourself more of these kinds of treats during the next few weeks.

- **Indulge yourself with extra time (and possibly money) on a favourite hobby or interest.** But be careful to choose one that doesn't hold too many memories of your past relationship – an interest that your ex-love didn't share would be ideal.

- **Each week for the next month, treat yourself to a small present that you *want* rather than just *need*.** It doesn't have to be highly expensive. You are buying it for its symbolic significance more than anything else. Choose something which you can keep in a place where you will see it everyday or something that you can wear frequently. Show your presents to friends and your self-esteem will be even further reinforced. (Good ones usually tell us how much we deserve to be spoiled!)

STEP 8

Put your heartbreak into perspective

Now you have reached the final essential step in our healing strategy. Anything else that you may do will be a bonus. Once you have succeeded in putting your heartbreak into perspective, you will have enough emotional stamina to carry on living without worrying about the negative aspects of heartbreak on your health or your capacity to manage your life – for example, your ability to earn a living or be a good parent and friend. (Our steps in Stage 3 are about *thriving* after your heartbreak rather than just surviving it.)

Although you may still be sad in your inner heart, you should now be feeling relatively positive and energized on a day-to-day basis. You should feel well able to face the world and function quite normally (for you) at work and in social situations. If not, you must backtrack through the healing steps we have discussed so far until you can. Perhaps you have pushed yourself too quickly or, alternatively, maybe you have more than an average amount of stress and hurt with which to contend. There are no prizes in this game for reaching the winning post early, so take as much time as you need.

The emotional state of grief can warp our sense of perspective. Our heartbreak can come to seem disproportionately important in relation to the rest of our lives. It can also warp our view of ourselves and our potential, as we tend to see ourselves as much weaker than we really are.

During this stage in the healing process you need to take action which will help you to see what has happened in a broader context of your whole life and your personality. Up until this point your loss has probably been taking up more of your time and energy than a) it deserves, and b) you can actually afford to give it. This may sound a harsh judgement, but in my experience it is almost always true. If we don't accept this as a fact, the danger is that we end up resenting the fact that we ever had such a wonderful relationship in the first place. So one of your main aims for this step is to be able to genuinely feel and accept that famous wise saying:

> 'It is better to have loved and lost than never to have loved at all.'

Another one of your aims is to open up your heart to the possibility of helping others who have been hurt or who are currently in distress. (Whether we like it or not, while our heart is broken, an automatic damper is put on our ability to feel for others, and we have much less energy and motivation to give to being a helper.)

Your final aim is to become aware of how much wisdom you have gained from the whole experience of having loved and been loved in return, and from eventually having your heart broken.

**Love is a wonderful thing,
but as long as it is blind,
I will never be out of a job.**

JUSTICE SELBY, DIVORCE LAWYER

Real time in this relationship

How long ago relationship started
3 Years 9 months = **1367 days**

Total time spent at work
(45 hrs × 48 wks × 3.75)/24 = **338 days**

Total time spent with friends, family, gym etc.
(15 hrs × 52 wks × 3.75)/24 = **122 days**

Total time spent sleeping
(56 hrs × 52 wks × 3.75)/24 = **455 days**

Total time actually spent in relationship
(1367 – [338 +122 + 455]) = **452 days**

Assuming life expectancy of 80 years, this equates to only 1/70 of my life!

Action time!

- **In rough figures, calculate how much of your life has been spent in your relationship** (see page opposite for an example of how to do this). Approximately how many months or years did it 'consume' of your life? Next subtract the absences away from your loved one when you were still a couple (for example, time with other friends and time spent at work). Assuming that you will live to an average age roughly calculate the proportion of your life it occupied. Even people who have been in long-term relationships are usually surprised by how little of their life has actually been taken up with this relationship (a helpful awareness when you are feeling as though your whole life has been ruined or wasted because of your loss!).

- **List the negative aspects of your personality that your relationship fostered or brought out.** Beside each write a positive counter-statement about yourself to put each into perspective. For example:

I was too trusting – my trusting nature usually pays dividends in my life; my friends and colleagues appreciate it.

I was too dependent – I am well able to look after myself and successfully did so for many years before we met.

- **Talk to some other people who have had their hearts broken and share your experiences.** If you don't know anyone, read a novel or some autobiographical articles or stories on the subject. Notice how universal some of the feelings and reactions are across the ages and the cultures. (If you can't be bothered to search the library or bookshop, one of the many new gossip magazines would serve this purpose – they are full of stories about divorced celebrities finding true love once again!)

- **Think about what you have learned about the world, people, relationships and your own personality through the experience.**

- **Try to quantify roughly the proportion of pain and pleasure that the relationship brought into your life** (for example, ten years of pleasure and six months of pain).

- **Make a list of some memories you wish to forget.** Shred this list into small pieces and ceremoniously burn or bury it.

- **Note down six examples of happy memories which you wish to treasure and remember.** If you have photos or any small significant momentos of these experiences, put these together with your list. Place them in a safe place. (Your grandchildren may like to look at them even if right now you think you won't!)

- **Give your self-esteem a boost with a special treat** – one that does not depend on you being in a relationship. (For example, going for a massage, buying yourself a huge bunch of your favourite flowers, filling the fridge with food that makes *your* mouth water, or even just blasting the house out with *your* (not your ex's!) music.)

**We learn wisdom from failure
much more than success.**

SAMUEL SMILES

Stage Three

moving on . . .

The steps in this stage are mainly designed to prepare you for your re-entry into the world of love and relationships. I understand that some of you may not feel like entering a new relationship, but I would suggest that you still work through this last stage. It will certainly not do you any harm! We will be looking at ways you can reinforce your personal strengths, build your self-reliance and have more fun. There are also steps to help you renew your faith in love and prepare a contingency plan in case you should meet another setback or hurt. So at the very least it will help you renew your trust in the world and yourself even if you decide to 'go it alone' after all.

Action is the antidote of despair.

JOAN BAEZ

STEP 9

Strengthen your strengths

You are so much more than a heartbroken individual.

The aim of this step is to fix this fact more firmly into the forefront of both your conscious and your unconscious mind.

During and immediately after heartbreak we are rarely functioning at our best. You may, for example, have become clumsy, forgetful, and less sensitive and understanding of others. At work it is likely that you have been 'surviving' rather than excelling. Perhaps your appearance and your home have begun to look less cared for than they usually are. All these are both very common and understandable reactions in the early stages of your loss. But it is important not to let these reduced standards become entrenched as habits. This is so easily done, partly because others often reduce their expectations of us at the same time. (Even though they may be being protective and kindly towards us by, for example, not expecting us to take so much responsibility at work or around the house.)

The danger when we are under-functioning for an extended period of time is that our memory starts to play tricks on us. We may actually forget how capable or attractive we used to be! The result is that our self-confidence plummets.

A period of making a conscious effort to play on your strengths and highlight your best personal qualities and features will rebuild your self-esteem and also give others a timely reminder of the un-heartbroken you!

Of course, ultimately, *you* are the best judge of whether or not a) you are under-functioning, and b) whether you are ready to give yourself more of a challenge. But sometimes you may need some help to arrive at your judgement. You may need some prodding forward from a good friend or, much more importantly, you may need to *experience* the evidence! Before being convinced, remember that you will need to *see* yourself looking more attractive, *hear* yourself talking excitedly about new goals and plans, and finally, *feel* the satisfaction of greater achievement.

But first things first! If you are going to test the water, you need your strengthened strengths to support you. Here are some suggestions to help you do this. So forget your weaknesses for a while (you can work on those later if you need to). Your aim right now is to reconnect with your inner strength and your skills.

> **Take strength in the fact that you are unique and the 'package' of qualities and skills that you have to offer the world is also unique.**

**Knowing is not enough, we must
apply. Willing is not enough,
we must do.**

GOETHE

Action time!

- **List three of your attractive PHYSICAL FEATURES** (and yes, you do have at least three!). Choose one or more of these to give some extra attention or care. For example:

  Hair – have a new cut or colour / give your hair a rich conditioning treat
  Legs – tone muscles in gym and then soak their tension away in a long warm bath / massage with moisturizing lotion / tan with self-tanning cream
  Facial complexion – treat yourself to a facial / enrich with a face mask

- **List three of your CHARACTER STRENGTHS and choose at least one to 'exercise'.** For example:

  Caring – ring your parents to see how they are / take the new office junior to lunch and find out how she/he is settling in / offer to cut the lawn for your elderly neighbour
  Sense of humour – go to see a comedy at the theatre / rent a funny movie / write a comic poem or story

Organization – plan a party or outing / revamp your filing system / tidy your cupboards and take any items you no longer want or need to a charity shop

- **Choose one of your INTELLECTUAL QUALITIES to give some extra stimulation to.** For example:

Problem-solving – treat yourself to one of those posh puzzles sold for executive desks / do more crosswords / buy a new book on a subject you've wanted to learn about for ages *Memory* – start learning a new language / learn a poem or song by heart / enter and practise for a pub quiz

- **Choose one of your WORK SKILLS and/or HOBBIES that you enjoy and are good at and give it some extra time.** For example: increase your networking to forge new contacts / plan a new project / draw or paint a picture / compose a short tune / do some DIY around the house / rejoin the football team.

STEP 10

Reinforce your self-reliance

Whether you decide to stay single for the time being, or you feel ready to start looking for another relationship, this step is essential. The advantages of being confident in our ability to fend for ourselves are obvious if we are going to be living on our own, but not everyone appreciates how vital it is to the success of a relationship as well. Research shows that the more independent couples can be of each other, the more likely their relationship is to survive. Of course, there may be times (such as during child-rearing or when one person is studying) when some financial dependency is inevitable and even advisable. But there is never an excuse or reason for any other kind of dependency.

For a good relationship to flourish and grow, we must not NEED the other person to enable us to:

- **feel good about ourselves** (for example, our self-esteem shouldn't leap into crisis if our partner criticizes us or dislikes our latest hairstyle). We should be making the best of our appearance and looking after ourselves well, for *ourselves*, even when we are alone.

- **cope with the outside world** (for example, we should be able to fend off unwanted salespeople, or deal with accountants and lawyers).

- **manage the day-to-day tasks of living** (for example, we should be able to do, or know how to get help with, house maintenance, cooking and ironing).

- **be motivated to achieve** (for example, we should not need to be 'nagged' to stick to action plans or be doing something just to please our loved one).

- **have a great social life** (for example, we should not need anyone else to find us friends or accompany us to restaurants or parties).

- **change our mood** (for example, we ought to know how to cheer ourselves up when things go wrong or calm ourselves down when we get overexcited or frightened).

It often isn't until a relationship breaks up that we realize how 'unhealthily' dependent on the other person we have been. So, if any warning bells were ringing while you were reading the list above, you need to spend some time now firming up your self-reliance.

> **For a relationship to flourish and grow, you need to be self-reliant.**

The best place to find a helping hand is at the end of your own arm.

SWEDISH PROVERB

Action time!

- **Give yourself at least two extra experiences of solitude per week**, but make sure that these are nurturing experiences. So prepare lots of treats such as your favourite food or a special video if you are at home. Also, take yourself off to places where you might expect other single people to be out happily on their own. For example, special gardens, galleries and museums. (I know many happily married people who prefer to go on their own to such places because they can walk around at their own pace and think their own thoughts without interruption, and I often join them!) Or search out certain cafes which are regularly full of people looking very contented as they munch their way through delicious meals with a good book or newspaper for company. (But steer clear of candlelit bistros for a while!)

  Keep up this 'treatment' until you no longer feel lonely when you are by yourself. (It will happen and you will enjoy it!) The more positive experiences of solitude you have, the less anxious you will be when you find you have unplanned periods alone. Remember, your brain simply needs training. At the moment it probably associates being alone with pain – you have simply got to train it to associate solitude with pleasure.

- **Firm up on your assertive skills so you can say 'no' when you need to do so,** and ask clearly and directly for what you need and want. Whenever you can, prepare and rehearse what you want to say or think you might need to say beforehand. This will help you to keep your requests sounding punchy and give a boost to your confidence. Use 'low-risk' situations such as public cafes or nights out with good friends to practise saying a plain and simple 'No, thank you' without giving unnecessary excuses. Remember to *look* relaxed, use a strong positive-sounding voice and make direct eye-contact most of the time.

- **Practise your anxiety-control techniques.** Make sure that you can quickly take control of your fear response. Experiment with various forms of relaxation techniques (see page 57 for a quick and easy relaxation exercise) until you find the one that works most efficiently for you. Then practise it daily.

- **Practise a technique and note down some other strategies for cheering yourself up when you get a dose of the blues.** The visualization exercise on page 36 would be a good technique to use. But also write down a number of activities you know lift your spirits. For example, watching your favourite comedy or action video; going to a football match; playing with your own or someone else's children; playing a game of golf or squash; going fishing or sailing or surfing, or spending a weekend at a health farm or at a guesthouse by the sea.

- **Make a list of at least three instant 'self-esteem boosters' that do not depend on others**, or you might even prefer to give yourself in private. These could include, for example:

  - using your mind's eye to visualize yourself enjoying a past success rather than

immediately phoning a friend when you
need moral support

– making yourself your favourite meal to
eat stretched out on the *whole* sofa with a
great video or book

– completing a much-needed chore at your
own pace and without unwanted advice
and put-downs, such as 'About time too!'

– giving yourself an indulgently long facial
and body massage without feeling embar-
rassed about your bulges and spots.

Inoculate yourself against loneliness. Give
yourself some mega-doses of pleasurable
time on your own – you will never fear
solitude again!

STEP 11

Give yourself an extra dose of fun

Hopefully when you were reinforcing your strengths in Step 9 you were also having some fun doing it and you have, therefore, quite recently been experiencing the healing power of fun. In recent times, the world of mental health care has woken up to the importance of bringing fun activities into treatment. Patients and clients are now just as likely to be prescribed dance, drama, juggling and music workshops as pills and work experience. Some psychologists and psychotherapists have even become specialists in laughter and in the UK the National Health Service has sponsored clinics offering this special kind of therapy.

More recently the world of physical medicine has begun to follow suit. Fun activities, they have discovered, have great benefits for health. The more of it the patients have, the quicker they are likely to heal and build up their resistance to future disease. This happens because laughter counters the effects of physical stress and the endorphins that it produces boost the immune system.

At the same time, many successful businesses around the globe have been profiting from the benefits of bringing more fun into the workplace. Comedy stars are not just used for after-dinner speeches, they are now regularly used for serious training purposes as well. Participation in sport and other fun activities are not just encouraged for staff relaxation purposes, they are routinely integrated into staff development programmes and planning sessions. Making the workplace a more fun place to be helps people maintain a positive outlook, work faster and think more creatively. It also acts as a social glue which keeps the workforce loyal and committed. ('The team that plays together stays together.')

Both the world of health care and the world of business use fun in these calculated ways because it is such a powerful human energizer. Furthermore, having lots of it makes economic sense. Health and the 'bottom line' improve.

Don't you also deserve a dose of the kinds of benefits that fun has been proven to bring?

It can be tough medicine to take though, especially when many of your normal fun activities probably have associations with your loved one. So start with small doses of fun and don't let anyone try to force-feed you with more than you know you can take at the moment. You may need to try new ways of having fun to begin with, and then return to your old sources when your heart is even stronger.

> **You deserve a generous dose of fun – and your broken heart *needs* it!**

**The most thoroughly wasted
of all days
is that on which one
has not laughed.**

NICHOLAS DE CHAMFORT

Action time!

- **Ring a positive, fun-loving friend and ask for suggestions of new ways to have some fun.** (It is understandable that you yourself may be devoid of any good ideas at the moment.)

- **Spend some time with young children.** Even if you don't have any of your own, they are not hard to find! Children's sense of fun is very simple and *very* infectious.

- **Go to a laughter workshop if there is one taking place near you.** Your local health service or library should have details. Readers in the UK could contact the Happiness project in Oxford who run excellent workshops. See the *Further Help* section at the end of the book for details.

- **Buy or borrow books and tapes which give you lots of permission and encouragement to have more fun.** Robert Holden's *Laughter Is the Best Medicine* or Ann Kipfer's *14,000 Things to Be Happy About* would be great starts.

- **Place some books of comic poetry and verse, or humorous short anecdotes, by your bed and in the bathroom.** Dip into them before going to sleep, on waking and when relaxing in the bath. These are all-important times for influencing your sub-conscious and will help set you in fun mode. Your brain will then be more likely to notice the fun opportunities that come your way.

- **Seize every opportunity for fun and enjoy it.** Be spontaneous and as the popular saying encourages, 'Go with the flow'! Don't hold back because the opportunities that arise, including dates(!), may seem frivolous or superficial, or a waste of time.

STEP 12

Start to believe
in love again

Hopefully your fun experiences have dented any cynical armour you may have put around your heart. But it wouldn't be surprising if there weren't still a few more layers of self-protection to work through! By now you have probably become quite adjusted to your new situation and feel relatively comfortable being on your own. Maybe you have never been so independent and are sensing the freedom that this can bring. You could even be singing the praises of solitude and wondering how on earth anyone could prefer to be restricted within the confines of a close one-to-one relationship.

This is a common stage in the healing of heart-break. And I do not deny it is a wonderful one! I have been there myself a number of times in

**To fear love is to fear life,
and those who fear life
are already three parts dead.**

BERTRAND RUSSELL

my life and still relish the memories. But what prompted me to move successfully and happily away from this stage?

I don't think it was simply meeting Mr Right. I think it was more to do with the fact that I was *ready* to meet him. (With no offence to my wonderful husband, there are after all millions of Mr and Ms Rights out there!) I was ready because I had been through all the healing stages we have looked at so far and now could accept that I had not just lost the person I loved, I had also lost a lifestyle I loved. At the core of this lifestyle was one close intimate relationship. Apart from the obvious sensual pleasures that were always 'on tap' (!), I enjoyed having a soul mate easily at hand to share small everyday pleasures and notice and respond to the more subtle shades of my moods. I loved the quiet, silent companionship you get from being with someone who you don't have to impress or entertain. I loved the kind of dinner parties where you can talk yourselves silly with other couples about family and home issues which would bore the singles to tears. I loved the nights of relaxed sensual dancing with other happily entwined couples. I loved having someone to surprise me with little gifts of a book or music they *knew* I would like, and I loved having someone with whom I could repetitively reminisce about the past and daydream unrealistically about the future.

That was what I still wanted and needed – even though I had also been so badly hurt by the relationships that had so far given me these pleasures. But, I am aware that some of you may eventually decide that you would prefer to remain single, for the forseeable future at least. But before you do dismiss the option of loving again, why not try to renew (or refresh!) your faith in love. It will do you no harm and could be very healing.

In this step you may notice that I have not suggested that you attempt to forgive your loved one for any hurt they may have inflicted on you. This is because **I do not believe that forgiveness is an *essential* part of emotional healing.** It has been my experience that trying and failing to forgive someone has stopped many unfairly hurt people from moving on. Forgiveness is a wonderful BONUS, but it may be an unrealistic goal especially in these relatively early stages of recovering from heartbreak. A much more realistic goal is to renew your faith in intimate close relationships, which has a similar healing effect. It reduces anger, bitterness and cynicism, which can be heavy burdens for you to carry. Holding on to such feelings can also make it difficult for you to relate to people who feel differently to you, and it can prevent you from enjoying many cultural and social experiences which have romantic love at their heart.

But this process, which I call 'Forgiving love itself', can be more challenging than it sounds. You cannot make yourself want something overnight that you may have been fearing and putting down for the last few months, or possibly even years. But take comfort in the fact that it is never too late to start believing in love again.

> **It is never too late to start believing in love again.**

**Love isn't what makes
the world go round.
Love is what makes the ride
worthwhile.**

FRANKLIN P. JONES

Action time!

- **Swop your comic bedside and bathroom books for volumes of love poetry and verse and dip into them as I suggested in Step 11** – before going to sleep, on waking, and while relaxing in the bath. (These are all-important times for influencing your subconscious.)

- **Take a trip to your local bookstore or library and stock up on novels and stories on the theme of love** – but make sure that they are not too sentimental and that the majority of them have a happy ending! Convincing quality love stories do exist! Ask for suggestions from friends and experienced librarians and booksellers, and search the book reviews for recommendations. My favourites are Louis de Bernieres' *Captain Corelli's Mandolin* and Jane Austen's *Pride and Prejudice*. Switch off the news and disaster-filled soaps and curl up on the sofa and read instead.

- **Take yourself (on your own, but with a box of tissues!) to the theatre or cinema to see romantic plays and movies.** Avoid any other

kind for a few weeks. Alternatively, rent
romantic videos to watch at home.

- **Spend time with neighbours, colleagues
  and friends who have a happy, loving
  relationship.** As a single person, you may have
  to make an effort to do this. I know many
  divorced and separated people find that they
  lose contact with friends with whom they used
  to socialize. One of the reasons this happens is
  that couples are often afraid to ask people they
  know have been heartbroken to spend time
  with them because they think it will rub salt
  into their wounds. Sometimes they feel that
  they can only invite a single person if they also
  invite another single as well. You may have to
  reassure them that you are now emotionally
  repaired and have a lot to gain from just being
  with them. (You can add that at a later date
  you may well welcome any chance to meet
  other eligible singles!)

- **Treat yourself to some new romantic music
  and love song albums and play them over
  and over again.** If you find that doing this
  brings back memories that are still very

painful or make you angry, retrace some of the healing steps you took earlier before attempting to move forward. (For example, allow yourself time to release your feelings, give yourself some treats and take some more comfort from a compassionate friend.)

**Take away love and
our earth is a tomb.**

ROBERT BROWNING

STEP 13

Decide what you want

Once you feel that your hurt and anger are no longer your dominant emotions, you are ready to start looking at what you want to do in terms of the future. For instance, do you want to remain single for the foreseeable future, or are you ready to start looking for a new relationship? And if so, what kind of relationship are you looking for and with what type of person? People who have had their heart broken are often reluctant to do this. Even though they may have regained their sense of power and control over their working life, they may still feel powerless in relation to their personal life. This is especially true if they feel that the break-up had very little to do with them, and was certainly not what they had planned or wanted.

Once the 'what' is decided,
the 'how' always follows.

PEARL BUCK

Of course, we cannot ever be in total control over the way our lives progress. Other people, accidents and illness are just a few examples of how 'Life' can disrupt even our best-laid plans. (And let's not forget that sometimes these disruptions can turn out to be in our favour. They can present us with opportunities to meet people whom we might normally never have met, or give us insights into ourselves which might make us want to change our dreams.)

But given that there are limits to the 'power' of deciding what you want, in the vast majority of instances it does speed up the process of finding the right partner. You will not have to spend so much time 'looking' because your search will be much more focused. In addition, you will not have to spend so much time healing your heart because you will 'weed out' most of the unlikely contenders before you have time to become too emotionally involved.

You will notice that I have not included a section on personal appearance in the following action points. You may think that is odd because this is the way (whether we like to admit it or not!) most people start looking for love. I believe that this habit is responsible for too many hurtful mistakes and lost opportunities. In fact, I nearly lost out on my own big chance for this reason! My second husband, to whom I have been happily married for 20 years, looked totally different from the outer image of the man I had in my mind when I started hunting! But he matched almost all other aspects of the profile I had in my mind for my 'ideal partner'.

Appearance is relatively easy to modify (and improve!). Other qualities such as basic personality, attitudes, values and expectations of intimate relationships are much more difficult to change. In the long run these are what count for so much in happy successful relationships. These are the qualities in people and the relationship you should be checking out on your very earliest dates. (Yes, you can do this! You just need to be observant and assertive enough to ask the right revealing questions.)

Know what you want and go for it with passion and optimism – but always keep your eyes wide open for exciting surprises.

**Nothing happens unless
first it is a dream.**

CARL SANDBURG

Action time!

- **Complete these sentences as many times as you can,** without thinking too long or hard before writing:

    - *I believe that I should always be* … (for example, honest, kind, fair)
    - *I would like to be remembered for being* … (for example, successful at my work, a good friend, fun to be with, a good parent)

    Study the sentences you have just written and notice which values keep reccurring. Try to list these in order of importance to you.

- **Using the above exercise as a guide, list in order of importance the 10 VALUES you admire most in other people and the way they lead their lives.** For example:

    1. Honesty
    2. Courage
    3. Ambition

- **Complete the following sentences as many times as you can,** without thinking too long and hard before writing:

  - *I love people who ...* (for example, make me laugh, work hard, are sexy and romantic)
  - *I hate people who ...* (for example, are boring, never have time to listen, have a big ego, are loud, are doormats)

- **Using the sentences you have just written as a guide, list in order of importance the 10 PERSONALITY CHARACTERISTICS you admire most in people.** For example:

  1. Kind
  2. Interesting
  3. Fun-loving

- **Complete the following sentences as many times as you can,** without thinking too long and hard before writing:

  - *I believe relationships work best when ...* (for example, the two people respect each other, are different to each other, put each other top of their priority lists, are not too dependent on each other)

- I'd hate to be in a relationship ... (for example, which is safe *but* boring, where one person is more dominant than the other, where each 'lived in the other's pockets')

- **Practise asking the right questions to get interesting strangers to start revealing their personality characteristics, values and attitudes** – it will help you to 'weed out' unlikely contenders before you become too emotionally involved.

How to Get that Interesting Stranger to Start Revealing!

- **Oil the wheels with very safe small talk first.** Even weather chat can be full of clues. (For example, some people keep themselves so busy they don't notice it; others get easily irritated when it is not perfect.)

- **'Test the water' by indirect questioning.** This is the gentle art of making comments designed to prompt a revealing response if and when the other person is ready and willing to oblige. For example, *'These conferences seem to get bigger every year. I'm surprised that so many people can still find the time to come. I suppose they must find them worthwhile'* is better than directly plunging in with *'What do you do and why are you here?'* or *'Do you like being in such large crowds?'*, and so forth.

– **Reveal before you probe.** Self-disclosure is the most effective way of getting others to disclose. For example:

'I love parties – but I prefer the ones with only 20 or so people so I can really get to know everybody – what's your ideal size of party?'

'This sun is reminding me of my holiday last month. I had a week in ___. It was perfect weather for chilling out – although the hotel was not that relaxing. Too big and busy for my liking. But I suppose that is what a lot of people want from their holidays – what's your ideal holiday spot?'

- **Use humour to lighten the interrogation! But be careful of jokes until you have got a few steps closer. A light humorous touch to the small talk and self-disclosure is what is needed first. For example:**

  'Oh, I forgot to buy my lottery ticket again – I suppose that's saying something about me. Although I wouldn't say 'no' if someone handed me a fortune on a plate, I can't be that bothered about being a multi-millionaire or I'd make sure I didn't forget. How about you? Do you play the lottery or do you have a much more interesting and dependable way of making money?' **[with the appropriate smile!]**

**Sometimes we make
the right decision
and sometimes we have
to make the decision right.**

DR PHILLIP MCGRAW

STEP 14

Get prepared for every contingency

Now that you are buoyed up by your strengths and hopefully excited about the prospect of finding love again, it is time to face the possibility that you might get hurt again. Perhaps you are still all too aware of this. You wouldn't be human if you weren't trembling a little inside. As you have already found out to your cost, the love game can be a risky business. When it goes wrong, it can hurt our hearts, our health, our work, our bank balance, our children, our relatives, our friends and our peace of mind. And to make matters worse, there are no guarantees and no insurances to be had!

No wonder some people are frightened off the love pitch for life!

Hopefully, you are not. If you have been working through the steps in this book, you should have reached a stage where *at the very least* you want to explore the possibilities again. You will know there are risks, but **you will also believe that the winnings are worth the gamble.** This step will show you how to make this gamble easier to live with. Instead of blindly entering the fray without a care or a thought about the things that could go wrong, you will go marching in with your eyes open and your mind prepared for every contingency you, as a mere mortal, can currently think of.

First, you will need to explore and confront the worst case scenarios. Then you will have to look at ways you can control the emotions that will result, and thirdly, you will need to plan what you can best do to rescue yourself and repair any damage that might have been done.

I have also included in my suggestions a couple of exercises to help you prepare a contingency plan for times when your emotional pain may flare up once again. I hope this does not happen too often for you, but there is a chance that it will on certain occasions such as anniversaries and holidays.

It's tough work facing the possibility of more pain, so why not give yourself a rest and a special treat now before reading on and launching yourself into action. You will do it more effectively if you do. Not only will you have more energy, you are also likely to have much more motivation and confidence in your ability to bounce back from any setback that might be thrown your way.

**Courage is rarely reckless or foolish
... courage usually involves
a highly realistic estimate
of the odds that must be faced.**

MARGARET TRUMAN

Action time!

- Note down who you could turn to for support should you encounter problems of confidence when you start to date seriously again.

- Note down three ways you could restore your self-esteem if on a date someone was critical of you or said they did not want to meet up again. (For example, remind yourself of a recent compliment; tell yourself that you have a right to be respected in spite of your imperfections and mistakes; promise yourself a compensatory treat.)

- Note down how you could take control of your feelings if you find yourself becoming over-emotional. (For example, do some deep breathing exercises / give yourself a treat / do a positive visualization exercise, such as the one on page 36 / go to the gym or go for a run.)

- Mark in your diary the dates which you know might revive some of the hurt of your

heartbreak (for example, important anniversaries, visits to memory-laden locations, your birthday, and so forth). Think about a small treat that you could give yourself on each of these days.

- **Note down other events which might trigger off the pain again** (for example, meeting a 'look-alike', your first sexual encounter with a new person, hearing certain music). Think about what you could do either before or afterwards which would help you to handle the situation.

- **Put this book, together with any others which you know could help you, in a convenient spot**, so that they are readily at hand to dip into should your heart need to be healed again.

You only learn to love by loving.

IRIS MURDOCH

A final word

I hope that you are already feeling healed and courageous enough to risk your heart again. If so, I wish you the very best of luck in your search for a new partner. (And yes, let's not forget that luck as well as effort can play its part in shaping all our destinies.)

But I am also aware that a fair number of you might still be feeling cautious or uninterested. I certainly wouldn't like anyone who had read this book to feel a failure if, on reaching its final pages, they were not raring to love deeply again. Perhaps, if that is where you are right now, what you need is a break from intimate relationships – and from books on how to manage the fall-out from them! Should your break prove to be long-term or last a lifetime, I hope that you also encounter plenty of luck in your search for alternative ways to enjoy life and make use of your precious potential for giving love.

A final word for those of you who might think you are 'past it' or too world-weary! Think of Nelson Mandela happily enjoying his eighties with a new love in his life.

Late in my life, I am blooming like a flower because of the love and support of her.

NELSON MANDELA

Further help

Recommended reading

Jane Austen, *Pride and Prejudice* (Penguin Books, 1994)

Louis de Bernières, *Captain Corelli's Mandolin* (Minerva, 1995)

Eileen Campbell, *A Dancing Star: Inspirations to Guide and Heal You* (Thorsons, 1992)

Jack Canfield, et al, *Chicken Soup for the Single's Soul: Stories of Love and Inspiration for the Single, Divorced and Widowed* (Health Communications, 1999)

Kristen Couse and Tom Dyja: *Heart: Stories of Learning to Love Again* (Marlowe & Company, 2001)

Bob Deits, *Life After Loss* (Fisher Books, 2000)

Stephanie Dowrick, *Forgiveness and Other Acts of Love* (The Women's Press, 1998)

Robert Holden, *Happiness Now!* (Coronet, 1999)

___, *Laughter, the Best Medicine* (Thorsons, 1993)

Barbara Ann Kipfer, *14,000 Things to be Happy About* (Workman Publishing, 1994)

Gael Lindenfield, *Assert Yourself* (Thorsons, 1986)

___, *Super Confidence* (Thorsons, 1989)

___, *The Positive Woman* (Thorsons, 1992)

___, *Managing Anger* (Thorsons, 1993)

___, *Self Esteem* (Thorsons, 1995)

___, *Self Motivation* (Thorsons, 1996)

___, *Emotional Confidence* (Thorsons, 1997)

___, *Success from Setbacks* (Thorsons, 1999)

___, *Confident Children* (Thorsons, 2000)

___, *Shortcuts to: Getting a Life* (Thorsons, 2002)

___, *Shortcuts to: Making Hard Choices Easy* (Thorsons, 2002)

Gael Lindenfield and Malcolm Vandenburg, *Positive Under Pressure* (Thorsons, 2000)

Peter McWilliams, et al, *How to Survive the Loss of a Love* (Prelude Press, 1993)

Ted Menten, *After Goodbye: How to Begin Again After the Death of Someone You Love* (Running Press, 2001)

Ray Mitsch, et al, *Grieving the Loss of Someone You Love: Daily Meditations to Help You Through the Grieving Process* (Vine Books, 1993)

Robin Norwood, *Daily Meditations for Women Who Love too Much* (Arrow, 2000)

Susan Quilliam, *Love Coach* (Harper Collins, 2000)

Useful internet sites

The sites below are just a *few* examples of well-established organizations in the UK which offer one-to-one support and a range of relevant talks and workshops. There are many hundreds of similar ones throughout the world. I would suggest you surf the Net first and then try to go to a talk so you can get a flavour of the way they work before signing up for long courses or one-to-one counselling.

Relate

www.relate.org.uk

Although this organization is primarily known for offering help to couples who want to improve their relationship, they also give excellent support to people who are trying to recover and learn from the break-up of a relationship.

Alternatives

www.alternatives.org.uk

Offers an interesting and uplifting programme of talks and workshops on aspects of emotional and spiritual health and development. It is a non-profit making organization in the heart of London. Although it is based in a church, it honours and welcomes all spiritual traditions.

The Happiness Project

www.happiness.co.uk

Offers a range of innovative healing and personal development workshops designed to inspire and support people who want to make changes in their life. A great deal of emphasis is placed on helping participants to develop a sense of inner joy and re-stimulating their sense of fun.

Cassettes

Gael Lindenfield has made a number of personal-development tapes. Each is designed as a self-help programme of exercises to be used on a regular basis. The list of titles includes:

Self Motivation (Thorsons, 1997)
Self Esteem (Thorsons, 1998)
Success from Setbacks (Thorsons, 1999)
Managing Emotions at Work (Thorsons, 1999)
Emotional Confidence (Thorsons, 2000)

These cassettes are available at all good book-shops, or direct from Thorsons (telephone 0870 900 2050 or 0141 306 3296).

About the author

You can contact Gael Lindenfield through her publishers at the following address:

Gael Lindenfield c/o Thorsons
HarperCollins*Publishers*
77–85 Fulham Palace Road
Hammersmith
London W6 8JB
United Kingdom

Or you can contact her directly by email:
lindenfield.office@btinternet.com

For further information about Gael Lindenfield and her current programme, go to her website:
www.gael-lindenfield.com